THE PORTLAND VASE
AND THE
WEDGWOOD COPIES

THE BARBERINI OR PORTLAND VASE

From a 19th century print

WOLF MANKOWITZ

THE PORTLAND VASE AND THE WEDGWOOD COPIES

ANDRE DEUTSCH

FIRST PUBLISHED 1952 BY ANDRE DEUTSCH LIMITED
12 THAYER STREET · MANCHESTER SQUARE · LONDON W1
PRINTED IN GREAT BRITAIN BY
TONBRIDGE PRINTERS LIMITED · TONBRIDGE · KENT
COLLOTYPE PLATES PRINTED IN HOLLAND BY
L. VAN LEER & CO. LTD·LONDON & AMSTERDAM

CONTENTS

LIST OF PLATES

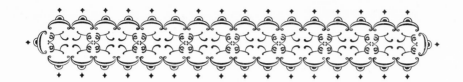

INTRODUCTION

THERE have been many notes, monographs, articles, arguments and guesses about the Portland Vase and the Wedgwood copies of it, and most of them are by distinguished authors. The vase itself has remained, throughout these years of polemic and discussion, patched and guarded in the British Museum, perfect and sought-after in its Wedgwood reflection, aloof from all final explanation, a perpetual challenge to the imagination of the countless thousands who have seen it. It is probably the best known vase in the world, yet such definite information as is known about it has never before been collected into one volume. With the casual certainty men have of the familiar, it is remembered as a dark shape decorated with light figures, a distinct, slightly off-balance shape, a famous vase, the *Portland* Vase.

This book has been undertaken in the hope of informing that certainty, and perhaps, thereby, renewing interest in this small but remarkable part of our national heritage. It is also hoped that now, after many years of rumour, argument, and nonsense, the true facts concerning the brilliant copies of the vase which Josiah Wedgwood made, will enable enthusiasts for the superb wares associated with that name, to substantiate their enthusiasm for the great potter's greatest essay in potting.

Thanks are due to, especially, Mr Tom Lyth, Curator of the Wedgwood Museum at Barlaston, whose vast knowledge of Wedgwood has been freely placed at the disposal of the author, to Mr Bernard Ashmole, Keeper of the British Museum Department of Greek and Roman Antiquities, to the firm of J. Wedgwood & Sons Ltd, who have made their records available, to Mr Felton Wreford, to Mr John Tulk, D.L., J.P., and to Mr David L. Seligmann and Miss Barbara Mankowitz for their assistance in research.

May 1952   *Wolf Mankowitz*

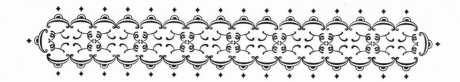

1

ON FRIDAY the 7th February 1845, William Lloyd, a young self-styled 'scenic painter', stepped out of the small crowd gathered round the Duke of Portland's Barberini Vase in the British Museum and achieved the only distinction of his life. He picked up a stone 'curiosity in sculpture' and cast it through the glass case, shattering to pieces the gem of the Græco-Roman Department.

Mr Hawkins, one of the Museum porters, heard the crash and hurried towards the crowd standing round the broken vase. He threw a terrified glance at the ruin, and asked what had happened. Lloyd stepped out of the crowd and said, 'I did it'. He would say nothing more and refused to give either his name or his reasons. He was taken, with Mr Hawkins and Sir Henry Ellis, the principal librarian of the Museum, to Bow Street to be charged before the magistrate, Mr Jardine. Remanded in custody for a week, at the end of that time he still had no explanation to offer. Sir Henry was anxious not only at the loss of a unique relic; he was also worried about the Museum's position with regard to the damage of objects on loan. No doubt Sir Henry would rather some higher authority informed the Duke of Portland of the fate of his treasured heirloom. For the destroyed Barberini had for years been considered, both in the public's mind and in the Duke's, as the 'Portland Vase'.

The life of an ancient *objet d'art* does not begin with its creation by an artist. Very often the artist is unknown, the period uncertain, the use or application of the *objet* a matter for speculation. An *objet d'art* is born when it is discovered, and its aristocracy is in no way dependent upon whether the place of discovery is a ducal palace, or a dung-hill. Its prestige is determined entirely by its æsthetic virtue, its perfection and its rarity. The beautiful but common-place can never enjoy a position of high caste among *objets d'art*, but the exceeding rare will not suffer by being less beautiful.

The Portland Vase has been considered by many to be inferior in shape and unimaginative in decoration, but its unique reputation and immense value as a perfect example of Greek cameo-glass have never been questioned. As an *objet* it has had a very long and distinguished life, though its origin – which will be considered later – is somewhat dubious and certainly obscure. Indeed, nothing about the Vase was ever quite so certain as its end, when it lay smashed to pieces by a neurotic young man from Ireland who could not hold his liquor. For although the Portland has been twice skilfully repaired since Lloyd's moment of aberration, a repaired *objet d'art* is a sad, reduced thing. Still rare, no one looking at it can believe it was once perfect. Its patched misfortune is, without intention, attributed to the thing itself; not only does its virtue suffer, but its price seriously depreciates.

Though Lloyd was charged with wilful destruction of an object valued at £1,000, it is more accurate to say that the Duke of Portland lost nearly ten times that amount through the scene painter's intemperance.[1] And Lloyd, who might have received a severe sentence for stealing the bottle of gin which led to his historic notoriety, could only be fined £5 or imprisoned for two months with or without hard labour. Furthermore (and this so infuriated a Fellow of the Society of Antiquaries that he wrote a letter to *The Times* demanding flogging for acts of vandalism), the British Museum had no grounds for taking any action against Lloyd. Mr Bodkin, for the Museum trustees, tried his hardest. 'There can be no doubt that in the eyes of the Law the prisoner has been guilty of wilfully and maliciously destroying this property and—' But Lloyd interrupted to say it was not done maliciously. Mr Jardine, who was as distressed as Mr Bodkin himself at the Law's failure to protect *objets d'art* of high caste, apologetically pointed out that Lloyd could only be convicted on a charge of breaking, *item* one glass case, the property of the British Museum. It was some slight compensation that Lloyd could not pay the £5 and was therefore assigned to the House of Correction for two months hard labour.

At his examination Lloyd created a surprisingly good impression by his dress, appearance, and the shamed manner and gentility of his statement. He refused again to give his name, but explained, 'my reason for refusing is simply this: that I do not wish to involve others in the disgrace I have brought upon myself'. He seemed almost eager to be punished; such a compulsive nature as Lloyd's may have harboured other and even darker impulses, for which he was glad to have gained correction. After all, not every drunk throws a curious piece of sculpture at a priceless vase.

---

[1] The Vase failed to find a purchaser when offered at Christies in 1929, which is not surprising in view of the reserve, said to be in the neighbourhood of £30,000. In 1945 it was bought by the Nation for an unspecified price.

'Whatever be the punishment you feel it your duty to award me, I shall have the consolation of feeling that it has been richly deserved,' he told Mr Jardine. No doubt he was just as disappointed as Mr Bodkin at the meagre two months the law produced out of its rag-bag of contradictions.

The common report that Lloyd was a madman – it is also said that he broke the vase with a stick – is not borne out by the facts. 'I certainly broke the vase,' he said, 'and all I can say in extenuation of my conduct is that I had been indulging in intemperance for a week before, and was then only partially recovered from the effects which that indulgence had produced upon my mind. I was suffering at the time from a kind of nervous excitement, a continual fear of everything I saw; and it was under this impression, strange as it may appear, that I committed the act for which I was deservedly taken into custody at the Museum.' It was with particular and suspicious emphasis that he turned to Mr Jardine and concluded, 'I can assure you sir, there was no malice aforethought, no design or evil intention whatever on my part towards any person.' Lloyd, as the doctors who examined him all agreed, was not mad. He simply needed to break something, and the Portland Vase was the closest thing to hand. If only he had been sipping wine at the time, he might have shattered his wineglass instead. But his fate, never very interested in his artistic ambitions, led him to the British Museum. His fate knew Lloyd well, for this was perhaps the only possible way in which he could have won a footnote in the pages of history; although he is still only a minor figure among those whose only contribution to art has been the destructive compulsion it evoked in them.

In Tothill Fields Lloyd angered the turnkey and, as a result, was handcuffed and put into solitary confinement. It is difficult to imagine him being obstreperous without cause, and perhaps solitary confinement was the only way he could think of to improve on the moderation the law had shown towards him. But he was doomed to pass out of the footnote he earned for himself as frustrated as he passed into it. After two days, someone paid his fine and he was discharged. He returned to the coffee house, and thence, one supposes, to Ireland and obscurity once more.

Following the calamity of 1845, antiquaries alternately fumed against vandalism and argued among themselves about the possi-bilities of restoring the Portland Vase; but the Duke himself[1] maintained an aloof silence. The Society of Antiquaries called a special meeting to consider the tragedy, and while Sir Henry Ellis thought restoration was not impossible, Mr Thomas Windus, whose monograph on the vase had appeared just after the tragedy had occurred in the Museum, thought it out of the question. Windus had attached an addendum to the end of his book, which suggests that he might have been the F.S.A. whose letter appeared in *The Times:*

'Just as this work was ready for the press, on the 7th of February, an individual, morbid with the organ of destructiveness, smashed this splendid specimen of Greek art into innumerable fragments. In common charity and good feeling let us drop tears on the catastrophe, and blot out the name of the perpetrator for ever; suffer it not for the sake of notoriety to be handed down to posterity as that of Eratostratus, the Ephesian, who burnt the famous temple of Diana, at Ephesus, on the day of the birth of Alexander the Great. The infliction of a severe public flagellation

---

[1] This was the 4th Duke of Portland. He had succeeded his eminent father (who was twice Prime Minister) in 1809. In 1810 the Vase was deposited with the British Museum for exhibition to the public.

for injuries committed on the fine arts would tend much to cauterise these phrenological mischievous sensations from breaking out into active violence.' Such are the caprices of time that in history Windus and Lloyd stand together, mere incidentals in the continuous story of the vase.

The antiquaries argued the points for restoration, one imagines, with much academic cross reference. But they were glad to inform one another that 'the late Giovanni Pichler, the eminent engraver of gems' had made moulded copies of the vase at Rome for Mr James Byres, and that the Marquis of Exeter, Mr Apsley Pellatt, and Mr Windus possessed copies. Mr Windus – whose sense of timing can in no way be considered deficient – observed that his own copy would shortly be exhibited, together with a plaster cast he had obtained of the sarcophagus in which the vase was found (*sic*) at the Polytechnicon.

James Tassie, the eminent Scottish medallist, is said to have taken copies from Pichler's mould in his famous glass-enamel body. But only Tassie plaster models of the vase are known, although Tassie medallions of some of its details are seen from time to time and were probably issued with his many other copies from the antique. The British Museum's own Pichler copy was at once put on exhibition to the public. 'The Vase by Wedgwood,' said Sir Henry Ellis, 'is only a modern copy, and not cast from the original.' Of course, Pichler's, Tassie's and Wedgwood's copies were all 'modern' – the difference between them being that Pichler's work was in soft plaster, in which definition and texture were quickly lost. Tassie's (assuming it to have been a glass-enamel copy) was taken faithfully from Pichler's, but in a solid white body, which made relief appear as an embossed decoration; and Wedgwood's copy, certified by Sir Joshua Reynolds as 'a correct and faithful imitation', had been worked on devotedly for four years by a team of men whose skill amounted to genius. It is obvious that later copies of the Portland Vase confused Sir Henry's memory of the first Josiah's work. However, two gentlemen named Doubleday and Baldock were set to work repairing the vase, using, presumably, whatever they could find for reference, and making an indifferent job of it.[1]

After the combined efforts of Lloyd, Doubleday (regarded by the *Gentleman's Magazine* as 'the prince of restorers') and Baldock, enthusiasts could only get an idea of what the vase had once looked like by examining copies of it. Most of these were of the quality associated with fairground trophies, the colours apparently chosen more out of consideration for the manufacturers' resources than for the qualities of the original. Furthermore, there were discrepancies between the material of which the vase had been made and the largely[2] pottery bodies in which copies were attempted. The original was of a deep blue glass, so deep in colour and opaque in texture as to appear black. Its surface had been coated with white glass, which was afterwards cut away to leave the decorative cameo, a feat of craftsmanship which Wedgwood thought had taken many years. Most copies followed Pichler and Tassie, and moulds were made from moulds which had themselves been taken from mould-copies. The fineness and clarity of line and the smoothness of finish which distinguished the Portland were thus lost in a crudeness which insulted everything except the ceramic skill of the copyists. Even the current Portland Vase copy which Wedgwood's had put out,

---

[1] The Vase was restored for a second time in 1948, after some missing fragments were found in a cardboard box among the effects of a Putney collector.

[2] Copies existed in plaster, brass, silver, iron, wood, marble and glass as well.

their 1839 version, was a moulded biscuit apology, in which the blue-black body was painted in. The particular characteristic of the 1839 copy is, however, the triumph of Victorian morality which it embodies. In it the figures, naked and austere in the original vase, are draped 'in the Greek manner', with a scrupulousness of which the Prince Consort himself would have approved.

The only copies to which those interested in the Portland could turn with confidence were the few put out by the first Josiah Wedgwood in the years 1790–96. These the most critical men of his time had examined and approved. They agreed that he had kept faith with the original. His copies were the only true and faithful replicas of a vase which embodied the classic ideals of eighteenth-century society.

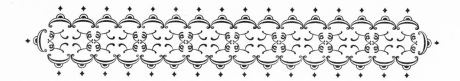

2

MARGARET, Duchess of Portland, died on the 17th July 1785. In 1786 Skinner and Co., auctioneers, of Aldersgate Street, had the pleasant commission of selling 'the contents of the Portland Museum, lately the property of the Duchess Dowager of Portland, at her late dwelling house in Privy Gardens, Whitehall'. The auction took thirty-seven days and the vase was Lot 4155, described in good faith as:

The most celebrated antique Vase, or Sepulchral Urn, from the Barberini Cabinet, at Rome. It is the identical urn which contained the ashes of the Roman Emperor Alexander Severus, and his mother Mammea, which was deposited in the earth about the year 235 after Christ, and was dug up by order of Pope Barberini, named Urban VIII, between the years 1623 and 1644. The materials of which it is composed emulate an onyx, the ground a rich transparent dark amethystine colour, and the snowy figures which adorn it are in bas-relief, of workmanship above all encomium, and such as cannot but excite in us the highest idea of the arts of the ancients. Its dimensions are 9 inches and 3 quarters high, and 21 inches and 3 quarters in circumference.

The story which makes Josiah Wedgwood the underbidder to the Duke of Portland is certainly untrue. The Duke gained the vase for 980 guineas and although Wedgwood was a buyer at the great auction, through his agent Humphreys, the items he wished to purchase were of no great importance, as the following letter[1] indicates:

Mr. Humphrey's Respects to Mr. Wedgwood, and acquaints him that he has bought the two Lots of China undermentd. in the Duchess of Portlands Sale, for him viz,

Lot 410——————£3 8 0
246   2 7 0

H. wishes to know if they are to be sent home, or if Mr. W. will send for them

Long Acre Friday 28 Aprl. 1786

Whoever his Grace's persistent and expensive competitor may have been it was certainly not Mr Wedgwood. If he was at the auction it seems more than likely that he was there to ensure that the Duke received his congratulations before those of any other ambitious potter. And so it must have been, for within three days the following document was drawn up:

I do hereby acknowledge to have borrowed and received from His Grace the Duke of Portland the vase described in the 4155th lot of the Catalogue of the Portland Museum, and also the Cameo Medallion of the head of Augustus Caeser being the 4153th lot of the same Catalogue, and both sold by auction by Messrs Skinner & Co. the 7th day of the present month of June

1 Wedgwood Museum Document, MS. 24881–33.

1786, and I do hereby promise to deliver back the said Vase and Cameo in safety into the hands of his Grace upon demand.

Witness my hand this 10th day of June 1786.

(Signed) Jos. Wedgwood.

Signed in the presence of

(Signed) Tho. Byerley.

In the same month Wedgwood, having spent some days making a detailed examination of the vase wrote to the distinguished connoisseur Sir William Hamilton, to ask his advice concerning the project of reproducing it. It is a letter of the utmost importance and deserves quotation in its entirety.[1]

Etruria June 24, 1786.

Sir

I thank you for your very obliging letter of the 23d of May, and shall ever retain a grateful sense of the kind partiality with which you have been pleased to honor my weak exertions. I cannot but feel myself highly flattered by the approbation of so exquisite a judge, who has himself introduced among us that pure taste, those elegant forms, which my humble studies have been employed in propagating and rendering permanent;— And the generous patronage and encouragement I have experienced in these pursuits, have carried me much farther than I had at first any idea of proceeding in them. You will be pleased, I am sure, to hear what a treasure is just now put into my hands, I mean the exquisite Barberini vase with which you enriched this island, and which, now that we may call it the Portland vase, I hope will never depart from it. His Grace the Duke of Portland being the purchaser, at the sale of his late

[1] Wedgwood Museum MS. E 18976.

[21]

mother's museum, has generously lent it me to copy, and permitted me to carry it down with me to this place, where I stand in much need of your advice & directions in several particulars, which I beg leave to state to you, for to whom can I apply with so much propriety or hopes of success, as to so able & willing a patron of the arts, of whose good offices I have already had such repeated experience, that I trust he will not withold them at a time when I stand more in need of them than ever, being engaged in an undertaking which appears more & more formidable upon every review of the charming original.

When I first engaged in this work, and had Montfaucon[1] only to copy, I proceeded with spirit, and sufficient assurance that I should be able to equal, or excell if permitted, that copy of the vase; but now that I can indulge myself with full and repeated examinations of the original work itself, my crest is much fallen, and I should scarcely muster sufficient resolution to proceed if I had not, too precipitately perhaps, pledged myself to many of my friends to attempt it in the best manner I am able. Being so pledged, I must proceed, but shall stop at certain points till I am favored with your kind advice & assistance.

It will be necessary however for you to know something of the powers I am in possession of for this attempt, before you can tell what advice to give.—I have several modellers constantly employed in the several branches of that art; and one of them, who was recommended to me by Sir Wm Chambers and Sir Joshua Reynolds, is esteemed the first of his profession in

[1] B. Montfaucon (1655–1741), *L'Antiquité Expliquée*, Paris, 1719. The vase is illustrated, inaccurately, Vol. 5, Pl. 19.

England. I need not add that I shall give myself unwearied attention to the progress of this great work.

The material in which I propose to make the copies, is much harder than glass, nearly as hard as agate, so that in this respect I have the advantage of my predecessors; and like the agate, it will bear to be cut, and take a polish, at the seal-engravers lathe. It has likewise a property peculiar to itself, which fits it perfectly for this imitation,—which is its taking a blue tint from cobalt, to any degree of strength.

It is apparent, that the artist has availed himself very ably of the dark ground, in producing the perspective and distance required, by cutting the white away, nearer to the ground as the shades were wanted deeper, so that the white is often cut to the thinness of paper, & in some instances quite away, and the ground itself makes a part of the bas relief[1]; by which means he has given to his work the effect of painting as well as sculpture; and it will be found that a bas relief with all the figures of one uniform white colour upon a dark ground, will be a very faint resemblance of what this artist has had the address to produce by calling in the aid of colour to assist his relief. That hollowness of the rocks, & depth of shade in other parts, produced by cutting down to the dark ground, & to which it owes no small part of its beauty, would all be wanting, and a disgusting flatness appear in their stead. It is here that I am most sensible of my weakness, & that I must of necessity call in the engraver to my assistance, in order to produce the highest finished & closest copies we are capable of making.

[1] '. . . the blue (glass) of the vase, when formed, and still red hot, was coated over, as far as the bas-reliefs were intended to reach, with the white glass, . . . the figures were afterwards produced in this coat by cutting it down to the blue ground in the manner of real cameos.'—J. Wedgwood, *Description of the Portland Vase*, London, 1790.

But in this resource difficulties arise, &, I fear, insurmountable ones; for how few artists have we in this branch whose touches would not carry ruin with them to these beautiful and high wrought figures? And suppose one or two could be found equal to the task, would such artists be persuaded to quit a lucrative branch of their profession, and devote half a life to a single work, for which there is little probability of their being paid half so much as they earn by their present employments; for I do not think £5000 for the execution of such a vase, supposing our best artists capable of the work, would be at all equal to their gains from the works they are now employed in; and the taste of the present age, you well know, Sir, is not awake, notwithstanding all you have done to rouse it, to works of much time and great expence. Here then I stand greatly in need of your assistance, for unless some new expedient can be happily thought of, we must submit to the loss of a beauty which we are perhaps capable of producing if all other circumstances were favorable to bringing it forward.

I suppose it is admitted, that the form of this vase is not so elegant as it might be if the artist had not been possessed of some very good reason for contenting himself with the present form,—either, perhaps, that he would engage the whole, undivided attention of the spectator to his sculpture, the vase itself being the production of another artist, of an inferior class, the verrier,—or, because the material made use of, under the circumstances necessary for the display of his art, that is, the body being made of one colour, and the surface covered over to a due thickness with another, was not capable of taking a form with those delicate parts on which its beauty as a simple vase would in great measure depend, and which might be given to a vase made of metal or other more manageable materials.

Now, though we should suppose the latter to be the case, I suppose you would still advise me to copy the form of the vase as well as the figures. But what I wish to ask you is, whether you would forbid me to apply these figures to any other form of a vase, or with the addition of any borders, or other ornaments.

I dare confess to you, Sir, that I have at times wrought myself up to a certain degree of enthusiasm, in contemplating the beauties of this admirable work; and in those paroxysms am ready to cry out, that this single piece is alone a sufficient foundation for a manufactory, & that of no small extent; and then I begin to count how many different ways the vase itself may be copied, to suit the tastes, the wants, & the purses of different purchasers.

The working artist would be content with a true & simple copy, a cast in one colour, of a durable material, with the price accordingly. Others, who could afford to proceed a step farther, would desire the addition of a blue ground, though painted only; and a third class would wish to have this addition in the composition of which the vase itself is made, & equally permanent, a fourth perhaps would pay for polishing this durable blue ground, and these two last would be my customers for Jasper copies; but whether any would be found with sufficient confidence in the abilities of our artists to order, or with patience to wait for, one of the highest order, finished by the engraver, or whether any artist would be found hardy enough to engage in it, I have my doubts. However, if you approve of the idea of making copies suited to different purposes as above mentioned, I will attempt one or two of the easiest first.

[25]

In examining the bas reliefs upon the vase, there appear a few palpable slips of the artist's attention, both in drawing and execution, as you have yourself no doubt observed. Would it be advisable in these cases, to make any deviation from the original, or to copy as close as we can its defects as well as its beauties?

Most of the figures have their surfaces partially decayed by time. When we mould from these figures, may we venture to restore their original smoothness, with care to preserve the drawing, &c.—or let the copies pass deficient as time has left the original?

I would next beg your advice respecting the introduction of these figures in other works and forms, in which they might serve the arts, & diffuse the seeds of good taste, more extensively than by confining them to the vase only. For instance, many a young artist, who could not purchase any edition of the vase, would be glad to buy impressions of the heads of the figures, or the whole figures, in a durable material of one colour, for studies. Others would purchase intaglios of the heads for seals, and cameos of two colours & polished grounds for rings, or the whole figures in separate pieces or groupes, finished to any degree, for cabinet pieces or pictures. In tablets for chimney pieces, & many other purposes, I have some reason to believe they will be acceptable, if I succeed tolerably in the copies. I should be glad to know if you see any objection to these proposed extensions & applications.

Several gentlemen have urged me to make my copies of the vase by subscription, and have honoured me with their names for that purpose; but I tell them, & with great truth, that I am extremely diffident of my ability to perform the task they kindly impose upon me; and that they shall be perfectly at liberty, when they see the copies, to take or refuse them; and on these terms

I accept of subscriptions, chiefly to regulate the time of delivering out the copies, in rotation, according to the dates on which they honour me with their names.

One word farther, & I have done. I have just now executed an order, by the direction of a merchant in Manchester, for an assortment of my Jasper ornaments with blue grounds & white figures, which he tells me are for the King of Naples. If so, you will perhaps see them in a short time, & I mention this to beg the favour of your correction if you think any of them worth so much of your notice. One thing I persuade myself you will observe, that they have been objects of very much labour & time, every ornament & leaf being first made in a separate mould, then laid upon the vase with great care & accuracy, & afterwards wrought over again upon the vase itself by an artist equal to the work[1]; for from the beginning I determined to spare neither time nor expence in modelling & finishing my ornaments, & I have the satisfaction to find that my plan has hitherto met with the approbation of my friends, for the purchasers of every nation declare them to be the highest finished & cheapest ornaments now made in Europe. I lamented much that I could not obtain liberty of the mercht. to send a vase, the finest & most perfect I have ever made, & which I have since presented to the British Museum. I enclose a rough sketch of it: it is 18 inches high, & the price 20 guineas. Mr. Chas. Greville saw it, & wished it was in his Majesty's cabinet at Naples.

Begging pardon for this long intrusion, I have the honor to be &c

The sketch of the vase could not be got ready for this post but shall be sent soon:— Subject, the apotheosis of Homer.

[1] This passage is an excellent description of 'under-cutting' in fine jasper-ware.

The conclusions Wedgwood reached through his detailed examination were many, but two stood out in importance. He discovered the true composition of the vase (it had been generally thought to be chalcedony or some similar natural body) and consequently that his task would be infinitely more difficult to accomplish than he had imagined – for the problem involved in persuading ceramic to appear as glass was formidable in itself. And he calculated that even if the artists were to be found with the genius necessary to reproduce the gem, the vast work of experiment would hardly be covered by a fee of £5,000. There was, of course, no one except Wedgwood himself prepared to find such a fee.

Sir William Hamilton's 'kind advice' is as important as Wedgwood's request for it. Hamilton's reactions typify a connoisseur and member of the Dilettanti Club[1], and he had, furthermore, been the second British enthusiast to own the vase. Though Sir William had sold it to the Duchess of Portland he had to no extent lost his admiration for the unique gem, as is shown by the following letter to Josiah, dated July 1786:

It gives me much satisfaction to find that the Barberini Vase not only remains in England, but is in your hands, as I well know that no one can make a better use of it. The person I bought it of at Rome will do me the justice to say, that the superior excellence of this exquisite masterpiece of ancient art struck me so much at first sight, that I eagerly asked, 'Is it yours? Will you sell it?' He answered, 'Yes; but never under £1000.' 'I will give you a thousand pounds;' and so I did,

[1] A group of connoisseurs who met regularly to discuss 'Etruscan' art, as it was called. Reynolds painted a group portrait of the Club, which was exclusive, influential and friendly to Wedgwood's ambition of 'reviving the Etruscan arts'.

though God knows it was not very convenient for me at that moment, and the business was concluded in a moment. Except the Apollo Belvedere, the Niobes, and two or three others of the first-class marbles, I do not believe that there are any monuments of antiquity existing that were executed by so great an artist; and I have no doubt of this being a work of the time of Alexander the Great, and was probably brought out of Asia by Alexander, whose ashes were deposited therein after his death. You have seen so well into the difficulties you will have to encounter, if you attempt an exact copy of this vase, that I have really nothing to add to the reflections you have made on the subject, and I much approve of your beginning with the most simple copies; and I much approve likewise of your making copies of single figures, and even of the heads; in short, you cannot multiply this wonderful performance too much, but I am convinced, as you say, that an exact copy of the vase, finished by the engraver, would be too expensive to find a purchaser in Europe. I admire your enthusiasm on the frequent and close examination of the vase, and am happy that its superior merit is felt by some few in England. I saw it every day for above a year, and protest I admired it more and more. You are very right in there being some little defects in the drawing; it would, however, be dangerous to touch that, but I should highly approve of your restoring in your copies what has been damaged by the hands of time. The side where the female figure has a torch reversed is perfectly preserved, and the other should be made as like it as possible. I should have thought my friend Flaxman would have been of use to you in your present undertaking; for I must do him the justice to say, I never saw a bas-relief executed in the true simple antique style half so well as that he did of the Apotheosis of Homer from one of my vases, and one of which you were so good as to send me. . . . If you could instead of sky blue, make your ground look like an onyx, as in the vase itself, it would be better, for there is no natural stone of the sky-blue colour. Unless you hold up the Barberini Vase to the light, it appears to be of a real onyx, and was long mistaken for one. I most heartily wish you success in your present arduous task. Follow your own judgement, for I am sure no one can see clearer into the merits of the original and the difficulty of copying it than I do. I think with you the form might be more elegant, and I would try one more elegant, but it must be simple.

Fortunately, Wedgwood did not take very seriously Sir William's concluding suggestion that the shape might be made more elegant. He decided to copy the vase in all particulars of form, colour, and design, and only to make good deficiencies which could be held due to the ravages of time.

The twelve months that followed were spent in endless discussions between Wedgwood and his principal modeller, Henry Webber, on the question of decorating the vase. At the same time at least two of Wedgwood's best artists, William Wood and William Hackwood (who modelled the famous portrait of Wedgwood himself) were engaged on the drawings and designs. In June 1787 the work on the figures and the final set of working drawings were completed. Wedgwood had spared no effort or expense to complete his preparations in the twelve months for which the Duke of Portland had lent him the vase. There followed three years of systematic potting and firing, experiment after experiment, sometimes ending in complete failure, sometimes advancing one step further towards the desired end. In July of 1789 Wedgwood was reasonably advanced in the task, but his standards of perfection were not yet satisfied. He wrote to a client in Bayreuth, that everything was proceeding satisfactorily, 'except the Barberini Vase which I have not yet finished in the manner I wish to do'. And then to Lord Auckland, Ambassador at Madrid: 'The prospect now brightens upon me, and after having made several defective copies, I think I begin to see my way clear to it'.

In 1790 Wedgwood wrote to his son Josiah the following account of his work on the Portland Vase:

Greek St. May 9. 1790

2 Trials of Barberini black. with respect to color, they are very much alike, & both very nearly the same as the vase I have with me. But in another respect, the total absence of cracks on the surface, that made of an equal mixture of blue and black, and then dipt in black, has the preference very greatly. It is indeed entirely free from cracks, which the other is not; and as it seems to agree perfectly with both your whites the yellow & the blue white, I would have you proceed with that in order to lose no time, & be getting more raw materials prepared. I think Dan Hollinshead & his brother should be kept entirely on the vase. For I have 20 copies subscribed for now, but this is only for yourselves, & must not be mentioned at the works for obvious reasons, I mean, that you should not mention its being greatly approved of, or many copies subscribed for—only let them go gently & steadily on with that as with any other work. But though I would have you be going on with this composition which we know will do, I wish you at the same

time to be making trials with the blue clay, to make it take a black dip without cracking; perhaps a little 59, or some ball clay, may have that good effect. The cracks are exceedingly minute, not visible when dry, even with a magnifying glass, but when the piece is wetted, they become distinguishable just before it is quite dry, by their deeper colour, the cracks retaining the water longer than the sound part of the surface.

I wish you to look at the left leg of Pluto between the calf & the ancle the latter of which is not seen, & compare it with a cast out of the mould taken from the vase itself which you will find in one of the drawers of the cabinet closet, this part is said to be too broad. If so, it must be narrowed a little.

Another deficient part in the vase I have is rather owing to accident, from the extreme thinness of the part, I mean the ham & upper part of the calf of the figure entering into Elysium, being jagged.

You had better agree with Dan. Hollinshead, as he seems to be come to his senses, & is an old servant. I can make Woodhalls place where he is as good as that you have promised him.

Some of the vases may be made with the white without any blue in it, & some with the yellow white, as I know that difft. people will have different tastes.

The theory I proceed upon with respect to cracking is this, that the black diminishes more in the burning than the blue, and therefore must crack if it keeps applied to the blue in every part. As 59 mixed with blue will cause it to diminish in burning proportionably to its quantity, to a certain degree, there is a proportion which will make it diminish exactly the same with the black; that proportion is to be found out, & the cracking is cured. I congratulate you on the success you have had in making one body, the mixture of blue & black, perfect in this respect— as also on your success in curing the enamel kiln, which is a very great acquisition.

Mr. Byerley says, & I join with him, that you will do anything you attempt[1].

Mr. Webber leaves this place to return to Stafforsh. on Tuesday[2].

At this point, the concluding stage in the creation of the Wedgwood Portland Vase, Wedgwood explained his problem to Hamilton thus:

to give those beautiful shades to the thin & distant parts of the figures, for which the original artist availed himself of the semi-transparency of the glass, cutting it down nearer and nearer to the blue ground, in proportion as he wished to increase the depth of shade. But the case is very different with me. I must depend upon an agent, whose effects are neither at my command, nor to be perceived at the time they are produced, viz., the action of fire on my compositions; a little more or a little less fire, and even the length of time employed in producing the same degree, will make a very material difference in this delicate operation.

In this respect perhaps complete success was impossible. Even the man who carved the original Barberini had occasionally allowed small mistakes to remain in his work, for it is certain

[1] The quality and promise of Josiah Wedgwood II as a potter are obvious from these remarks, and are worthy of observation because of the tendency for this talented man to be overshadowed by his father's genius.
[2] Wedgwood Museum Document, MS. E 18993–26.

that in the hand-carving of such a design upon so difficult a medium as glass, minor slips of the gem-cutting instruments would produce effects not calculated by the artist.

In all artistic creation there is observable a conflict between the medium – the clay, the stone, the paint or the words – and the intention of the artist. Wedgwood's materials were mud from a hole in the ground. They never possessed the natural virtue of marble, or granite, or glass. Whatever beauty a Wedgwood vase possessed was imparted to it by the mind, hand and civilisation of men. Wedgwood's Portland Vase began its life as a little dirt out of a quarry somewhere in the Midlands of England, and whatever happened to it after that was ceramic history – written impeccably by one of the most gifted hands of his age.

A 'first good copy' was finished in October 1789, and Wedgwood sent it to Erasmus Darwin at Derby. Darwin's enthusiasm for the work of his friend was such that he ignored a specific request that the vase should not be shown, and brought several of his friends to see it – 'not', he wrote, 'cognoscenti, but philosophers', implying therebye character differences which are not so clearly defined in our own day.

Once Wedgwood had discovered the technical means to produce a perfect copy, it was possible for him to go ahead with the first edition. In spite of the temperamental difficulties of the kilns, the vagaries of heat in firing, and the tendency of the jasper bodies towards incalculable behaviour, he could now embark on a programme, supply the clients who wished to order copies, and recoup some of the expense his experiments had involved. In a general sense then, the first edition of the Wedgwood Portland Vase dates from 1790. In that year too the vase was shown to Queen Charlotte, whose admiration and support for Wedgwood had made him her potter in 1765. There is a letter extant from M. de Luc, the Queen's personal secretary, dated 5th May, 1790.

M. De Luc presents his compliments to Mr. Wedgwood; he was very sorry to be obliged to go to Windsor the day that Her Majesty had appointed to see the Vase which pleased her very highly. He was come today to try to repair his loss; and he had taken the liberty of bringing with him Mr. Thom Willis (son of the Dr.) and Mr. Andr. De Luc his nephew. It might be difficult to him to meet again with these two Gentl. to come together another time; therefore he takes the liberty to beg Mr. Wedgwood the favour, in case they come without him, to shew them the Vase.

Throughout April and May the copy Queen Charlotte had found so highly pleasing was publicly exhibited at Wedgwood's showroom in Greek Street, Soho. Numbered the fifteenth example of the first edition, the copy was certified by Sir Joshua Reynolds, President of the Royal Academy:

I can venture to declare it a correct and faithful imitation, both in regard to the general effect, and the most minute detail of the parts.

(Signed) J. Reynolds

Leicester Fields
15th June, 1790.

It was also examined and applauded for its truthfulness to the original by the Duke of Portland himself, the Earl of Leicester, President of the Society of Antiquaries, and Sir Joseph Banks, Bt., the gifted dilettante who had accompanied Captain Cook on his Australian tours and was the greatly respected President of the Royal Society. With so much interest at such high levels, the whole of London society wanted to see Wedgwood's Vase, as it was already being called. It became necessary to issue tickets to view the vase and nineteen hundred were printed and distributed. The ticket, an aquatint of the vase by S. Alkin, is in itself important, being the first reliably drawn picture to be published[1].

In June, Wedgwood's son, the second Josiah, together with Thomas Byerley, Wedgwood's nephew and a partner (the great Thomas Bentley died in 1780) took No. 15 as the gem of a collection which they were to display in Holland. 'I do not know whether I have told you in so many words,' instructed Wedgwood, 'that you must not on any account part with the vase, but bring it back with you. It will be necessary to keep this identical one, that I may be able to confront gainsayers with it. We have not yet made one so fine as yours.'

In Holland, the obliging Lord Auckland's enthusiasm for Wedgwood's work gained the travellers an audience with the Prince Stadtholder and the Princess of Orange, while Lady Auckland gave a breakfast for them at which we may be certain everyone at the Hague who was either important or fashionable contrived to appear. In this atmosphere of distinguished patronage and high enthusiasm the peak achievement of a craft which was little more than a century old in England, the most refined work – so the age felt – ever accomplished in European ceramic history, and the personal triumph of England's greatest potter, brought an English industry to the foremost place. It was with his Portland Vase that Wedgwood completed the conversion of, as his monument in Stoke Parish Church puts it, 'a rude and inconsiderable Manufactory, into an elegant Art and an important part of National Commerce'.

[1] This is reproduced on p. 65. In 1791 excellent engravings were made of the vase, probably by William Blake, and were used in a Wedgwood catalogue of 1810

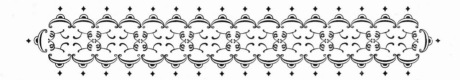

3

INTEREST in the Portland Vase was at its highest when Wedgwood opened his exhibit in Greek Street of copy No. 15. Many gentlemen were eager to subscribe for copies, and yet, paradoxically enough, it was not a commercial proposition for Wedgwood to undertake more orders than he could help. He had already shouldered the immense cost of experimenting in the jasper body in which the copies were made, and this expense he was always prepared to accept, not only for the sake of perfection, but for the experience he gained thereby in the production of jasper. But quite apart from this great and undischargeable burden, the cost of making individual copies of a quality Wedgwood was prepared to issue, was very high. He discussed it with the younger Josiah without much optimism – for how could his patrons appreciate the immense cost involved, and the technical problems of special firing?

I do not know what to say about the price. I have not yet been able to make another good one. I have tried five more since you left us, but not one near so good as that you have; so that unless we are more successful, £50 is too little to save us from loss. However, there is no appearance at present of it being at all prudent to fix the price at less than £50. What encouragement is there for us moderns to attempt the production of such works, if their patrons refuse to pay one-twentieth part of what the ancients paid to their artists?

Eventually it was decided to charge copies finished in the highest style at 30 guineas, and defective and less finished copies (in those special cases where their issue could be justified) at less. For the fine copies a case was made and charged at £2 10s. Finally a few copies were to be issued, where clients requested it, in blue solid body jasper, the cameo in white or yellowish-white, at a lower price.

So from the very start Josiah Wedgwood was inclined to make his edition of the Portland Vase as small as possible. The estimates which have been made of the number actually issued are entirely guess-work. Wedgwood never committed himself, for the best reason of all, to a definite figure. To do so would have been to involve himself in great capital outlay, depleting the resources his expanding industry required, and restricting the whole of his production programme because of the special facilities demanded by the manufacture of the copies.

It is however, from our point of view, important to try to assess as accurately as possible, the actual number of fine vases in Barberini black jasper, finished in 'the highest style', which constituted the important first edition. For this issue, a very much smaller one than has been reported, is the only Portland vase edition possessing the great quality and consequently the high value which is rightly associated with the finest work of Josiah Wedgwood. Important as these copies are to the Barberini, they are more important to the history of Wedgwood and Wedgwood ware.

The second Josiah Wedgwood, who had taken the first good copy, No. 15, to the Continent, wrote in 1839 a letter which is of considerable importance. In it he states that:

> the number of copies was restricted by the difficulties and risks attending the execution of each copy, which were so great that I believe my father never sold ten copies, and the moulds were not broken but are still in my possession.

But although the moulds were in his possession and unbroken, he did not attempt to put out a second edition in 'the highest style'.[1] In the few years after his father's death in 1795, it is certain that a few copies in both the blue jasper body and the black were finished off and issued. But however many copies the first edition comprised, they were all potted and fired during the life of the first Josiah, and are therefore important examples of his work, whether they are of the finest or of the second quality.

Bearing in mind the second Josiah's remark, that 'my father never sold ten copies' – several copies were presented, however, to friends and relatives, and to public institutions – we are fortunate in being able to refer to the oven books which were kept at the Etruria factory. These records cover the period succeeding the 'first good copy', No. 15, and they are our most reliable indication of the size of the first edition.

¶ *Extract from oven book, 27th May and 3rd June* 1791, *page* 31.
  6 Black jasper Barberini (Barberanean) Vases dipped.

---

[1] A letter dated April 1836 addressed to William Bell of Hull makes it clear that this was the case. 'The Vase', Josiah Wedgwood II wrote, 'was not entrusted to me but to my father near fifty years ago.'

6 Turned, 6 Finished, 6 came out of B. oven price paid for making 7s. and 16s. for doing over again each.

(Dan Hollinshead was 'the maker' and Hackwood the finisher.)

¶ *8th and* 15*th July* 1791, *page* 37.
    6 Jasper Barberini Vases.
        6 Turned, 6 Finished, 6 came out of B. oven; price paid same as before.

¶ *9th and* 16*th December* 1791, *page* 62.
    3 Black jasper Barberini Vases.
        3 Turned, 3 Finished, 3 came out of B. oven; price paid same as before.

¶ *6th and* 13*th January* 1792, *page* 65.
    6 Jasper Barberini Vases (Barberanean).
        6 Turned, 5 Finished, 5 came out of B. oven; price paid for them making & repairing them all over 16s. and 7s. each (16s. was for repairing them all over).

¶ *3rd and* 10*th February* 1792, *page* 69.
    6 Black jasper Barberini Vases.
        5 Turned, 5 finished, 5 came out of B. oven; price paid as before.

¶ *16th and* 23*rd March* 1792, *page* 74.
    2 Jasper (Black) Barberini Vases.
        (Both these reported to have been broken.)

¶ 13*th and* 20*th April* 1792, *page* 77.
> 6 Black jasper Barberini Vases.
>> 5 Turned, 5 Finished.
>> (Six are put down as having come out of oven.)

¶ 19*th and* 26*th December* 1794, *page* 202.
> 2 Jasper Barberini Vases.
>> (These are entered as being broken.)

¶ *Extract from Oven Book.* 1796. *Page* 5.
> 6 Black jasper Barberini Vase.
>> (These are entered as being broken.)

By this, the only reliable record of the black 'Barberanean' Portland extant, we see that not more than 30 copies 'came out' in all. If we assume that all the copies made up to the 'first good copy', No. 15, were not destroyed, we get a grand total of 45 copies, of which certainly no more than 31 could have been of the finest quality. The blue solid body copies are not listed in the oven books, being cheaper and of much less importance. We can therefore say that the first edition of Wedgwood's Portland Vase could not have exceeded 45 copies, inclusive of imperfect examples.

These first copies were not marked with the usual impress *Wedgwood* mark. Some of them were numbered inside the lip of the vase in manganese pencil, probably indicating the order in which they were fired rather than that in which they were made, or the subscribers for whom they were intended. The pencil mark where it occurs varies greatly in clarity. Before firing and while the vases were in the 'green state', being 'cheese-hard' or 'leather-hard', they were carefully *undercut* by William Hackwood[1] to strengthen their detail. The jasper body is of very high quality and offers a silken smoothness to the touch. The dimensions are approximately those of the Barberini itself, ten inches in height, and seven inches at its greatest diameter. The copies in the blue body are a little larger in their overall dimensions, and not as finely finished in the undercutting as the black. The variations in size are due to the difficulties of precision in potting, and the vagaries of contraction in firing.

The colour, 'Barberini black', gave Wedgwood much thought and experiment. The blacks vary accordingly, some of them containing barely perceptible blue elements, of which others are free. As Sir William Hamilton had pointed out, the colour of the Barberini appeared to the eye to be black, and could only be seen as blue when held up to the light. Wedgwood, who was under no misapprehensions at all about the entire difference in nature of ceramic and glass, satisfied himself with a black colour which would take a glossy finish when polished, bringing it as near as possible to the appearance rather than the actual material of the Barberini. This black he obtained by the twice dipping he describes in the letter to his son on page 31.

Thomas Byerley, whose carefully systematic character would have been a great asset to any business enterprise (his portrait shows him lugubriously intent, one feels, on balancing the accounts: he was also the father of fourteen children), made a list in his pocketbook of those who placed orders for the vase. We cannot, however, take this list as being very much more than an indication of interest in the piece; the 'copies received' and the clients 'acquainted' are less than half the total list:

[1] As described by Wedgwood in his letter to Hamilton, page 21.

Duke of Portland, two copies   Copies not received by 1800.

Lord Walsingham   Copy not received up to 1799.

Professor Copland, of Aberdeen.

Tho. Astle, Esq.

D. Braithwaite, Esq.   'London Dec. 19th, 1799.

Mr. Braithwaite says that in return for some South American Earthenware he gave the late Mr. Wedgwood, he was to have had an Etruscan Vase but Mr. Wedgwood afterwards said that if he succeeded in making the Barberini Vase and there should be one a little faulty, he should have that in lieu thereof, and he supposes it was on that account, Mr. Wedgwood had set his name down in the list of subscribers. He feels the delicacy of mentioning this and hopes it will not be misconstrued – if there should be a Barberini a little imperfect he will be very glad to receive [it] and thinks the intentions of his late friend will only thereby be fulfilled.'

Thos. Byerley to Josiah Wedgwood II.

Roger Wilbraham, Esq.

Lady Pepper Aiden   To be acquainted.

Earl of Besborough   Copy not received by 1801.

H.R.H. Prince of Wales   Copy not received 1807 when he visited Etruria and ordered six copies. Memo

[43]

	against order 'put by and waiting orders for delivery' and later 'to be sold'.
Phil. Stephens, Esq.	
Mr Fox.	
Dowager Duchess of Beaufort	Copy not received up to 1799.
Doc. Letsom.	
Lord V. Palmerston	Copy not received up to 1799.
Povie, Esq., of Tidsworth, near Salisbury.	
Thomas Hope, Esq., Amsterdam	Copy received 13th June 1793, price £31 10s. and Case, £2 10s. Now in possession of Josiah Wedgwood & Sons, Ltd., 34 Wigmore Street.
His Excy. John Trevor	Copy received 22nd December 1797. Price £27 11s., paid 12th February 1799. This copy is now in the Fogg Museum, as part of the Winthrop bequest and is numbered 9.
Baron Veltheim.	'Acquainted.'
Mr Rost.	'Acquainted.'
Lord Viscount Stormont.	
John Sneyd, Esq.	Copy received 3rd July 1797. Price £27 6s., paid 4th February, 1801.
General Stuart.	
Lord Auckland.	
Earl of Upper Ossory.	
Mrs Montague.	
M. of Landsdowne.	

Duke of Marlborough Copy received 28th April 1797. Price £33 12s. Paid 12th September 1799.

Lord Hawkesbury, no figure at bottom.

In addition to the above patrons, some of whose orders were filled, the following gentlemen are listed as having purchased copies – the quality of which may be deduced from the prices paid.

Earl of Mansfield	1799	Price £33	12s.	0d.
Edward Constable	1797	Price £31	10s.	0d.
Sir James Pulteney	1797	Price £31	10s.	0d.
Lord Viscount Lismore	1811	Price £17	1s.	3d.
Duchess of Würtemburg	1804			
Dr T. Beddoes	1799	Price £31	10s.	0d.

Further to these, the following copies were presented, those to the Darwin family being the gift of Wedgwood himself, and the rest being given by Josiah Wedgwood II.

Dr Erasmus Darwin Copy No. 12, still in the Darwin family.

Dr R. W. Darwin Copy No. 28, now in the Victoria and Albert Museum.
Dr Darwin wrote in 1793: 'I am infinitely obliged for your father's kind intention respecting the Portland vase, but should think myself sufficiently gratified in being allowed to have it on the terms mentioned in my last.'

British Museum, 1802.

French Republic, 1802 — 'Le Ministre de l'Interieur Salue le Sr. Wedgwood et lui accuse réception du vase de Barberini. Il le prie de recevoir le témoinage de son sincére attachment.

(Signed) Chaptal.'

Thomas Poole — Who wrote in 1802: '. . . the Portland vase for which am indebted to your brother.'

Museum of Edinburgh University. — A resolution of thanks was received from the Lord Provost, Magistrates and Council of the City, on 21st August, 1815.

In 1814, according to a letter addressed from the London showrooms by the careful Byerley, there remained of the first edition, '10 Portland Vases, 4 of them tolerably perfect, and 6 rather imperfect, having a leaf off or a few staines'. Of these some still remained fourteen years later, for in 1828 Mr Apsley Pellatt[1] wrote to Wedgwood's as follows:

Mr. Pellatt has called to see the Portland Vases and begs to know if he takes the whole at £120, whether you would engage to make them only for Messrs. Pellatt & Green what price per Vase, he also asked if he might take part at the prices fixed.

Mr Pellatt had been a keen middleman in the fine Wedgwood wares – in 1829 when the contents of the Wedgwood warehouse in York Street, St James's Square, were sold, he was a conspicuous

[1] Of the Falcon Glass Works, Southwark.

buyer – and he also had a fine personal collection of wares produced during the life of the first Josiah, and the best period of the Wedgwood and Bentley partnership. It is possible (especially since the last copies were hanging fire), that Mr Pellatt managed to buy them.

At all events, after 1829, it is not likely that any more original copies were sold. The great venture of the Portland vase copies, which began in 1786, had ended after more than 40 years.[1]

*   *   *

The following list of extant copies of the first edition of Wedgwood's Portland vase in Barberini black, is complete as far as can be ascertained. In each case the number quoted is the manganese pencil figure on the inner lip of the copy. The numbered copies are in all cases of more perfect quality than the un-numbered ones, but it is not possible to say with certainty what the numbers indicate.

No. 3   Barker copy.
No. 4   Falcke copy: in the British Museum.
No. 6   In Germany.
No. 7   Rickman copy: originally owned by Apsley Pellatt.
No. 8   Phillips copy.
No. 9   Trevor copy: Fogg Museum, Cambridge, Mass.
No. 11   Tulk copy.
No. 12   Erasmus Darwin copy.
No. 15   'First Good Copy': in the British Museum.
No. 25   Barlaston Museum copy: Josiah Wedgwood's.

[1] Invaluable information in this and the preceding chapter was first compiled by Mr John Cook, late Curator of the Wedgwood Museum, and published in *Old Wedgwood*, No. 6, 1939, by the Wedgwood Club of America. It has been extended by Mr Tom Lyth, present Curator, and by the author.

No. 27   Lady Lever Art Gallery copy.

No. 28   R. W. Darwin copy: Victoria and Albert Museum.

No. 29   Felix Joseph copy: in Nottingham Museum.

Hope copy: the copy sold to Thomas Hope of Amsterdam in 1793 may possibly be No. 2.

Other copies not numbered are:

Three copies, two blistered: A. Spero collection.

Two copies, one blistered, one incomplete: Barlaston Museum.

One copy, overshaded and faulty: Lady Lever Art Gallery.

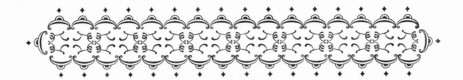

4

I T IS not unlikely that in the eighteenth century a princess belonging to an old and noble Roman family should have been addicted to gambling, and it is well known that fortunes which have been augmented by the turn of a card have been depleted by the same exercise. It is probable that in the event of serious losses a lady, even a noble lady, honourably determined to redeem her debts, would follow a feminine economy and realise on something other than her personal finery and the jewels which have always meant so much to her beauty. When the Princess Barberini needed money she cast a calculating glance in the direction of the famous Barberini Cabinet. And in spite of the Pope's specific direction that the glory of Rome should remain with that city, a gem of the collection, a vase which with its beauty and rarity had graced the Barberini name for many years, passed out of Roman hands. The princess redeemed her honour at no expense to her personal adornment. But the old capital of the world lost an important bauble when the Barberini vase left on the first stage of a journey that was to take it to a new capital and a new name.

That first stage was accomplished through the shrewdness and the fine knowledge of local conditions which characterised a

Scottish gentleman by the name of James Byres. He had lived for 40 years in Rome, collecting ideas and material in his profession of architectural designer. He was, furthermore, an antiquary whose reputation was greatly respected by the distinguished dilettanti of the great city. Byres it was who acquired the vase from the unlucky Princess Barberini, about the year 1780. What he paid the lady for it, he carefully does not mention, but if Sir William Hamilton is to be trusted in accounts of dealing – an occupation in which a degree of exaggeration is habitual at all levels – Byres sold the gem to him for £1,000. Hamilton was an enthusiast rather than an authority on ancient art, but in 1772 he had already sold his famous Porcinari Collection to the British Museum for £8,400. We may assume that he did not make a loss on the Porcinari, for he sold the Barberini in 1785 for 1,800 guineas, a good and speedy appreciation.

Lady Margaret Holles Harley, who married the second Duke of Portland in 1734, devoted a great deal of enthusiasm and much money to forming her own 'very curious' museum. Horace Walpole described the lady as 'a simple woman, but perfectly sober, and intoxicated only by *empty* vases'. In the frontispiece of the 1786 Sale Catalogue, the Barberini appears crowning a pyre of feathers, shells, fishes, and Roman remains. The drawing is not very accurate, but taken with Wedgwood's comment that Her Grace carried out the transaction with Sir William (through her friend, Sir William's niece, Miss Mary Hamilton) 'with such secresy (*sic*) that she was never known, even by her own family, to be the possessor of it', it suggests the great lady's eccentric turn of character. The Duchess doubtless had her reasons, but she was unable to keep the secret for long, for she died a year after buying the vase. Death which closes but one door, and opens so many, let the Barberini and all the Duchess's strange possessions out into the light of day. Walpole called the Museum 'not a tomb . . . but the treasury of the Duchess of Portland', and the amount that the auction realised must indeed have been considerable. There, as we know, the third Duke bought the vase back into the family possession for 980 guineas – Sir William had, it appears, paid a sound market price for it – and Wedgwood arranged to borrow and copy it. So that we know quite definitely, the successive owners of the vase from the Barberini family to the third Duke of Portland. But beyond this we know very little.

The account of the vase current in the eighteenth and nineteenth centuries, is that it was found in a sarcophagus taken from a sepulchral chamber beneath the Monte del Grano on the road to Frascati, in 1582. However, Flaminio Vacca the historian, describes, in some detail, the opening of the Monte del Grano,[1] and the objects discovered there, including the sarcophagus; but he does not mention the vase. Such a gem as the Barberini would hardly have been overlooked by an antiquarian. It is reasonable to assume that he does not mention the vase because it was not there.

In point of fact, the first occasion on which the vase was even remotely associated with the Monte del Grano was in Terzi's *Aedes Barberinae*, a history of the Barberini family and its relics. Terzi's account was published in 1642, and *à propos* the vase he recounts what must have been a family rumour (since historians must find reasons wherever it is humanly possible) that it was the cinerary urn of the Roman Emperor Alexander Severus and his mother Mammea and that it contained their ashes. As it was now generally supposed that the Monte del Grano sarcophagus was that of Severus and Mammea, Santa Bartoli in his work on

---

[1] Stuart Jones, in an article in *The Athenaeum* (1909) first pointed out this crucial fact.

sepulchral monuments, published in 1697, appears to have felt justified in putting two and two together, and deducing that the famous vase was found in the Monte del Grano. Bartoli's is the first reference to the vase being discovered in the sarcophagus. This observation, however, was made more than a century after the opening of the Monte del Grano and, so far as one can tell, without any evidence whatsoever.

The story that the sarcophagus was that of Severus and his mother, is also not proven, and seems extremely unlikely. Severus and Mammea were murdered in A.D. 235 by the Roman legions in Germany, and it is difficult to imagine even the most devoted of retainers taking the risk of bringing the dead bodies – assuming the ferocity of the soldiers had left anything of them – back to Rome for decent urn burial. Furthermore, Severus was twenty-seven when he died, and the male figure on the sarcophagus is of a much older man.

So, not only is it unlikely that the vase ever had anything to do with the Monte del Grano sepulchre, but it is almost certain that it had nothing to do with Severus either. This account concerning the source of the vase, though repeated for some three hundred years, is probably pure invention.

Furthermore, the quality of the glass of which the vase was made, together with the style of its decoration and the type of craftsmanship it displays, can now be ascribed to a period preceding the birth of Christ by fifty or sixty years. It was probably made by Greek craftsmen in the celebrated glass-manufacturing centre of Alexandria. In addition, it is certain that it was not made in the form in which we have it today.[1] The

[1] The date here and the suggestion regarding the original shape of the vase, are Mr Bernard Ashmole's – to whom the author is greatly indebted.

Auldjo Vase in the British Museum is of similar period and workmanship to the Barberini, and its standing base has a turned finish. On the other hand, there is an *amphora* in the Museo Nazionale di Napoli of a similar glass to the Auldjo and the Barberini, which though more ornately decorated than the latter, is like it in shape and style. The Neapolitan Vase – discovered at Pompeii – is of the shape more usual in *amphorœ* of this type. It terminates almost in a point, and below the level of the decorative panels is a frieze.

It seems, then, that Josiah Wedgwood's conclusions[1] concerning the famous carved base of the Portland vase were correct. He perceived that the glass was different in quality, and in the style of its decoration. In the base cameo, the mysterious figure in the Phrygian cap, the pupils and irises are carved. In the figures decorating the body of the vase this is not the case. The base – which is now displayed separately in the British Museum – is of later date. There is, in conclusion, the mark of careful chipping round the bottom of the white decoration on the vase, which suggests that, either because the *amphora* was broken or because the vase-shape was preferred, the lower part of it was cut away. The base was then cut out of another piece and inserted in accordance with an aesthetic sense inimical to that of the original period and culture of the vase.

So much may be observed with certainty of the vase itself. Quite uncertain, however, is the meaning of the vase and of the figures decorating it. It is possible, of course, that it has no meaning beyond being a beautiful work, damaged at some far off time, perhaps by a later Roman Lloyd, and then reconstructed and patched up by some connoisseur-artist who thought that, even if

[1] In his *Description*, 1790.

[53]

it lacked its original virtue, it would still be a beautiful thing to have about the villa.

To come to such a conclusion would give our story a reasonable, and balanced end. But for nearly four centuries people have speculated about the vase, and called their imaginative deductions 'interpretation', and it can be held that, insofar as a work of art may be said to have meaning at all, that meaning is as much what has been attributed to it as what was intended by the forgotten artist. At all events, there is no reason why we should not enjoy the 'interpretations' which have been made by distinguished gentlemen in the past, so long as we resist the temptation to become too highly interpretive ourselves.

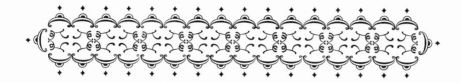

5

THE decoration on the body of the Portland vase falls into two
scenes. In them two central figures recur, and clearly depict
a story. In addition, the bases of the handles are decorated
with masks, and the base of the vase depicts a figure in *chlamys* and
Phrygian cap, with a finger raised before its mouth.

Now most of the interpretive theories of the nineteenth and
eighteenth centuries are greatly weakened by their assumption
that the vase was discovered in the Monte del Grano sarcophagus.
On this assumption, and on the surmise that the sarcophagus
related to Alexander Severus and Mammea, the decoration was
said to depict an allegory of the life of that emperor. When,
however, it was decided that, following known portraits of her, the
lady whose effigy surmounted the tomb was the Princess Faustina
and the man, the Emperor Marcus Aurelius Antoninus, it was
assumed that the ashes said to have been in the urn were
theirs. Marcus employed the services of that great physician
Galen, it is said, in the curing of his daughter of a mysterious
malady. Then, it was deduced by some, the *scena* represented the
before and after of the cure. It was 'an event or cure, on which
Galen valued himself most, the case of a noble lady who was said

to be in a very dangerous state, whose ailment he discovered to be love, the object of which was an actor or rope-dancer'. And there in the first scene, we see the lady, the torch of her life dipping towards the ground, languishing unto death. And on the other side the stern, thoughtful figure of the venerable Galen, looking on while the lady joins her hand with that of the actor, and Cupid hovers above, his torch rekindled.

It was an attractive theory, and one to which the known disposition of both Faustina and her daughter of the same name gave much support. They were both of them greatly appreciative of wrestlers, gladiators, actors, and other young men, and there was a recorded instance of one or other of them extending her affection towards a rope-dancer named Pylades.

But of course, the whole theory rested on the discovery of the vase in the sarcophagus. And we know that it almost certainly was not discovered there. Furthermore, one may ask, if the vase was a burial urn, why should it celebrate a family physician rather than the royal personage whose ashes it contained? For the cure redounded more to the credit of the great physician's insight, than it did to the libidinous fancies of the Roman lady. The whole of this theory, in fact, is inacceptable.

Thomas Windus, the antiquary whose monograph on the Barberini appeared at such a timely point in the vase's history, embraced the Galen suggestion, eagerly. Mr Windus enlisted the assistance of the Dowager Baroness de Rothschild in bringing over from Rome a plaster cast of the sarcophagus, and then proceeded to substantiate his belief that the vase celebrated Galen in every particular. It seemed to him that the stern and venerable standing figure in scene two of the decoration 'had a medical appearance, similar to that of Hippocrates on a coin of Cos.

I resorted,' he continues excitedly 'to the biographies of ancient Greek and Roman physicians. When I came to that of Galen, the whole allegory blazed on me at once in unison with my favourite hypothesis; from the excitement I exclaimed with all the ardour of Archimedes, *EUREKA! EUREKA!*'

But he had not got it at all.[1] Windus' guesswork led him to find 'face-skins' with leeches and bandages pendant in the formal masks on the vase handles, a whole allegory of Galen in the bas-reliefs on the sarcophagus, and perhaps – though the eminent fellow does no more here than suggest it – a cult in which Galen was virtually worshipped as divine, one in which flagellation, mutilation, and anatomical dissection – forbidden by Roman law – were carried on at an esoteric level. It was a startling theory for an early Victorian, and in his book Windus carried it much further than it could reasonably go. Alas, his theory depended on the vase having been in the tomb, and at the risk of becoming repetitive, we must say again; it almost certainly was not.

The other method of interpretation favoured by the classical scholars was no less imaginative. Many of them took part in a sort of lottery in which the mind fumbled in the ragbag of classical mythology, and pulled out a story which would more or less fit the figures on the vase. A mythographer named Pyl favoured the love story of Medea and Jason, while a certain Herr Klein preferred that of Theseus and Amphitrite. Montfaucon saw the serpent as a swan, and concluded that the story was that of Leda. Venuti considered it a version of the Judgment of Paris. De la Chausse, speaking for a whole school of interpreters, called it 'the congress of Jupiter Ammon with Olympias'. Bonada modestly suggested

[1] Except that his suggestion that the figure on the base represents Angerona, the secret deity presiding over the fate of Rome, seems reasonable.

that the figures 'excellently represent an apotheosis'. Terzi favoured the life and times of Alexander Severus; Fabretti agreed with Count Terzi, although he thought that the figure on the base represented the druid priestess who warned Severus against the Britons. 'Go,' she said, 'but neither expect victory, nor trust thy soldiers' – a depressing piece of advice to celebrate on a cinerary urn. A Mr Marsh told the Society of Antiquaries in 1784 that the two scenes contrasted 'the slothful, obscene, and libidinous' Heliogabalus with 'another Alexander, rival of heroes, patron of the Grecian arts, the emperor Severus'. But perhaps the scope and variety of the interpreters of the Barberini have already been sufficiently indicated. Clearly, nobody knew what it meant.

But although the paths of love were tracked differently according to inclination among the mythographers, they all agreed that the story in the *scena* was a tale of love. All of them, that is, except Miss Meteyard, the author of the first Josiah's *Life*. She preferred to believe that it was 'simply a heathen and poetised allegory of the trials of human life and its close'. In this case it may be said that Miss Meteyard was closing her eyes to the facts. But let the lady rest, for in her vast and adulatory researches, she made surprisingly few other mistakes.

Josiah Wedgwood, in his pamphlet on the Barberini vase, does not commit himself to a definite opinion, although in common with his age he assumes that it was found in the Monte del Grano, and that the sarcophagus celebrated Alexander and Mammea. Dr Erasmus Darwin, on the other hand, very strenuously demonstrated that the vase celebrated not an individual, but an entire ritual. He thought that it expressed certain of the Eleusinian mysteries, the fertility cult from Asia Minor with its enactment of death and rebirth. Darwin felt that the vase played a part in some latterday revival of the mysteries, and this theory is not as far-fetched as some of the guesses of his academic contemporaries. For if all the suppositions that have been made prove anything at all, it is that the story or statement on the vase is a mysterious and evasive one, not available to an observer whose esoteric knowledge is restricted to the familiar recital of the doings of gods and heroes.

For clearly it is a statement, though a concealed one which can only be unlocked if the key is found. And to make a statement in this way was precisely the method of the mysteries. The figure on the base may be Angerona, or it may be Hippocrates, but whatever else it is, it suggests silence in its gesture and in its pose. Furthermore, it is not difficult to imagine such an enjoinment to silence being fixed in the base of the vase for a ritual rather than a functional purpose – for, as many have asked, why place a cameo where it could never be seen? The obvious answer here would be, it sometimes would have been seen. It would be seen, for example, in a ritual in the course of which the vase was first suspended by its arms above eye-level. In that situation, the message of the vase would be *Silence and Secrecy*; perhaps some rite of initiation was then performed. Then possibly the vase would be lowered on to an altar and the initiates introduced to the mysteries enacted by the symbolical figures decorating it. The possibilities of the Darwin theory are the most exciting of all.

Mr King of Trinity College, Cambridge, an eminent classical scholar and art critic of the mid-nineteenth century, has the distinction of having his favoured theory of the Portland's mythological story, supported by the vase's most recent interpreter. In his description of the vase in the 1926 Catalogue,[1] Mr A. B.

---

[1] Of the gems in the Greek and Roman Department of the British Museum.

Walters states that the scenes represent a version of the Peleus and Thetis story. Classicists may recollect that in the earliest versions of this love story, Thetis changed into a horde of ravenous sea-monsters, at the point when Peleus, with more eagerness than tender address, bound Poseidon's daughter and attacked her with the urgency of his regard. Mr Walters suggests that on the vase we have a later version in which, typifying the more sophisticated and restrained taste of the time, the legend has been softened in its symbolism.

If this is so, then we can only remark with wonder a softening which reduces a horde of sea-monsters to a tame dog-headed serpent, and Peleus' eager lust to a quiet, trance-like approach to his pining beloved. In fact, the serpent symbol, and the venerable male figure in a posture which – though it had medical associations for Thomas Windus – is known to typify Poseidon, are the only elements in the design which suggest a sea-myth. Thetis, as is well known, was taken by guile rather than by her own desire for Peleus. And if Cupid with the torch, and the tenderly inter-locking arms, indicate anything less than mutual desire, then one must forget all the simple recognisable symptoms of love, and search for better and more appropriate myths.

This we may do, and with more or less success, depending on the broadness of our mythological terms of reference. But when we find, finally, the most fitting story of all, we must be prepared for the disappointment it will involve. No matter what names, of what gods and heroes, nymphs and goddesses, we settle on, the plot of our story will still be an archetype truth carved in strange terms and pure lines on an antique vase in the British Museum. Like all truth it will never be entirely available to our eager but limited comprehension.

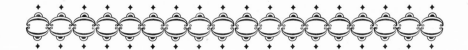

BIBLIOGRAPHY

Description of the Portland Vase, J. Wedgwood, London, 1790

New Elucidation of the Portland Vase, T. Windus, London, 1845

Life of Josiah Wedgwood, E. Meteyard, London, 1865

Handbook of Wedgwood Ware, E. Meteyard, London, 1875

Old Wedgwood, F. Rathbone, London, 1893

Josiah Wedgwood & His Pottery, William Burton, London, 1922

Catalogue of the Gems in the Graeco-Roman Department of the British Museum, A. B. Walters, 1924

Josiah Wedgwood, Samuel Smiles, London, 1894

Josiah Wedgwood, A. H. Church, London, 1903

Correspondence of Josiah Wedgwood, edited K. E. Farrer, London, 1906

Wedgwood Ware, Harry Barnard, London, 1924

Wedgwood's Copies of the Portland Vase, John Cook. (*Old Wedgwood* No. 6, 1939, published by Wedgwood Club of America.)

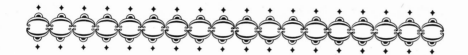

INDEX

THE BARBERINI VASE

Height: 10 inches

Widest girth: 6 inches

Body: glass upon glass

Colour: opaque dark blue appearing black, overlaid in shaded white

IN THE following plates, the Vase appears in its finally restored state and though the texture of the glass body is largely lost, the original shape is preserved.

Though the date and place of discovery of the Barberini are unknown, it was probably made at Alexandria, where Greek glass manufacture in the second century A.D. produced work of this quality.

The following letter is from John Flaxman to Josiah Wedgwood and is dated 5 February 1784. It appears to be Wedgwood's first introduction to the Vase.

'I wish you may soon come to Town to see Sir Wm. Hamilton's Vase, it is the finest production of Art brought to England & seems to be the very apex of perfection to which you are endeavouring to bring your bisque & jasper; it is of the kind called "Mulineux by plying" made of dark blue glass with white enamel figures, the base is about a foot high & the figures 5 & 6 inches engraved in this same manner as a Cameo & of the grandest & most perfect Greek sculpture.'

Plate I: The Barberini Vase

Plate II: The Barberini Vase

Plate III: The Barberini Vase

Plate IV: The Barberini Vase

THE HOPE PORTLAND

Height: 10 inches

Widest girth: 7¼ inches

Body: solid jasper

Colour: black with cameo in tinted white

THE following comments are from Josiah Wedgwood's *Commonplace Book* (pages 21–2, No. 28409/39, in the autograph of Alexander Chisolm, Wedgwood's amanuensis) and were made on comparing the copy exhibited in April–May 1790 with the Barberini. The remarks do not apply in all particulars to the Hope copy, which is without doubt the most perfect of all copies. They do, however, show the perfection sought by Wedgwood and the comparative points of interest to the connoisseur.

'Cupid – The inside of the left thigh is too shaded.

The young man in the portal – His left foot is too large. The straight line in his leg is rather too strongly coloured, and his arm and neck a little too much. . . . The female figure with the serpent – The mouth, that is, between the lips – and between the mouth and the chin, should not be coloured at all.

Pluto – The least shade in the world under his breast & on his left ribs. His left leg a little above the ankle, that is, from the calf to the ankle, rather swells out, but should diminish. . . . Mask heads – The shades are rather too strong. Leave the tongue fuller, broader, & the black part in the mouth narrower. . . . Female figure with the torch – the neck rather too much shaded, very little so. . . . The tree coming from behind the figure – its back leaves are too dark. . . . The breasts of the figures, and some of the muscular parts of the bellies, are rather too flat.'

The Hope copy is numbered obscurely on the inner lip, and is permanently displayed at the Wedgwood showrooms in London.

71

Plate V: The Hope Portland

Plate VI: The Hope Portland

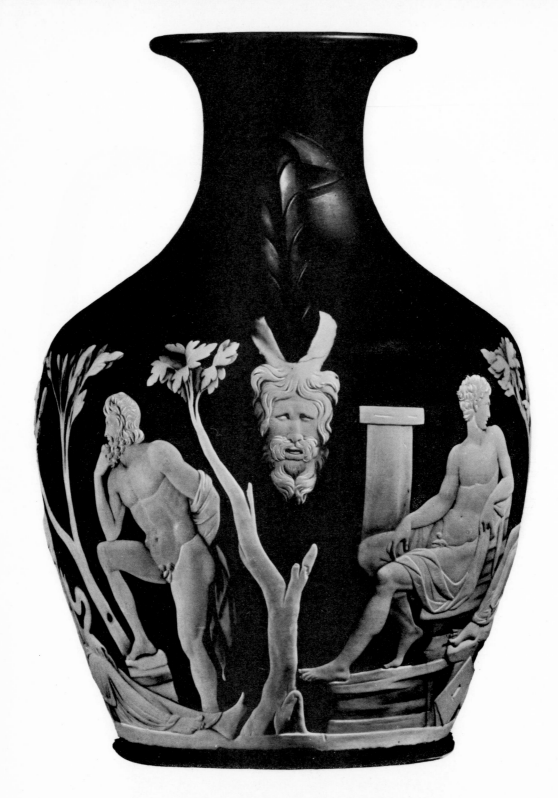

Plate VII: The Hope Portland

Plate VIII: The Hope Portland

THE NORTHWOOD PORTLAND

Height: 10⅛ inches

Widest girth: 7½ inches

Body: solid jasper

Colour: black with white shaded cameo

JOHN NORTHWOOD of Stourbridge was the first modern craftsman to make an exact copy of the Barberini in its original material, glass. Northwood's glass copy was shown in the rooms of his company, Perkes & Co., Stoke-on-Trent, in January 1877. At the same time Northwood was engaged by the Wedgwood firm to polish a pottery edition of the Vase. He had apparently been asked to work an edition of thirty Wedgwood copies, and wrote, 'I do not think I could do them under 1½ to 2 years and should not like to be tied to a month or so as I should like to turn out each one perfect'.

The records show that in fact fifteen Wedgwood copies were sold by subscription at Messrs W. P. & G. Phillips of Oxford Street.

The special mark of the polisher, a cyphered 'JN', is shown in the white relief above the impress mark Wedgwood. The Greek letter above the cypher may indicate the number of the vase. *Plate XIII.*

In spite of the remarkable quality of both the potting and the polishing in the Northwood, making it the most important of all the modern copies, a comparative examination will reveal its inferiority to the first edition as represented by the Hope, indicating the extra-ordinary degree of perfection in craftsmanship achieved by the first Josiah.

The Northwood illustrated is Wedgwood's own copy and is on permanent exhibition at their Wigmore Street showrooms in London.

Plate IX: The Northwood Portland

Plate X: The Northwood Portland

Plate XI: The Northwood Portland

Plate XII: The Northwood Portland

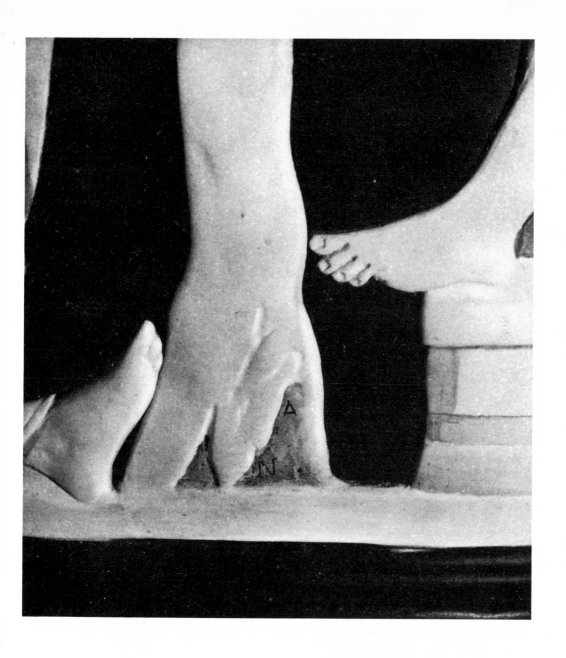

Plate XIII: The Northwood Portland

MISCELLANEOUS COPIES

Plate XIV: The Solid Blue Jasper Portland. This is the cheaper edition put out by Wedgwood at the time of the fine Hope quality issue. The number of copies issued in the blue body is unknown, but is not likely to be very high. A perfect specimen is in the British Museum. The copy illustrated is from the Tulk collection and is fire-cracked, although the cameo is in fine state and well finished.

Plate XV: The 1839 Portland. The general edition, first put out in 1839, is of inferior quality and is remarkable only for the drapery which Victorian taste added to the figures. Definition is blurred and modelling and potting are of low quality. The colour is either black or blue applied to the white stoneware or earthenware body.

Plate XVI: The Bellows Portland 1909. An inferior limited edition made for an American firm. The shape and quality are of very low order, and a distressing sheen envelopes the entire vase.

Plate XVII: The Ordinary Jasper Portland. The ordinary edition of which the copy illustrated is a black solid body example, was put out in all the jasper colours especially dark blue and black, both dip and solid, and in all sizes, from 1880 to quite recent years. This is the edition which is most commonly found and its quality is very uneven.

All these copies, with the exception of *Plate XIV*, bear the Wedgwood impress mark either on the rim of the base or on the base itself. They are between 10 and $10\frac{1}{4}$ inches high and are subject to slight variations, due to contraction in firing.

Plate XIV: The Solid Blue Jasper Portland

Plate XV: The 1839 Portland

Plate XVI: The Bellows Portland 1909

Plate XVII: The Ordinary Jasper Portland

THE PORTLAND BASES

The immense variation in the quality, finish, and modelling of the vases can be seen from the following comparative plates, which may be used with considerable reliability for determining the quality and period of Portland copies.

87

Plate XVIII

Figure 1: Barberini

Figure 2: Hope

Plate XIX

Figure 1: Northwood

Figure 2: 1839

Plate XX

Figure 1: Bellows

Figure 2: Ordinary

MOULDS AND IMPRESSIONS

Plate XXI. The original mould of the Portland Vase, preserved in the Wedgwood Museum at Barlaston. It was towards the completion of a perfect mould that Wedgwood engaged the services of his artists for the year during which the Barberini was on loan to him. It is this mould which has often in the past been alleged to have been broken by Wedgwood to maintain the scarcity of Portland copies.

Plate XXII. Some of the wax and plaster impressions produced in the course of copying the Barberini.

Plate XXI

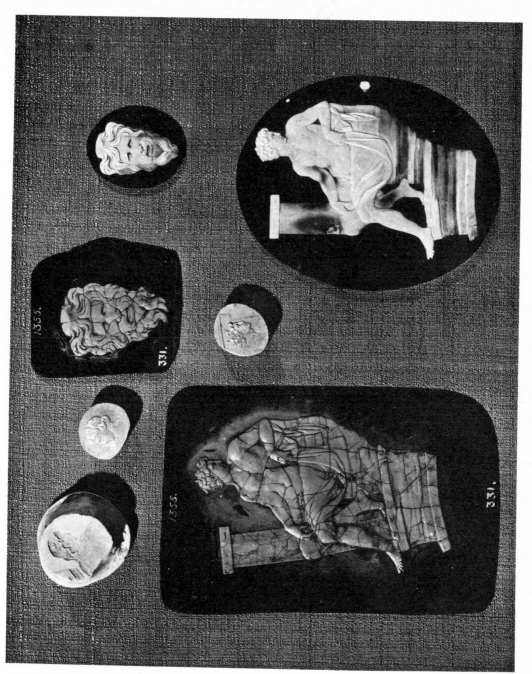

Plate XXII

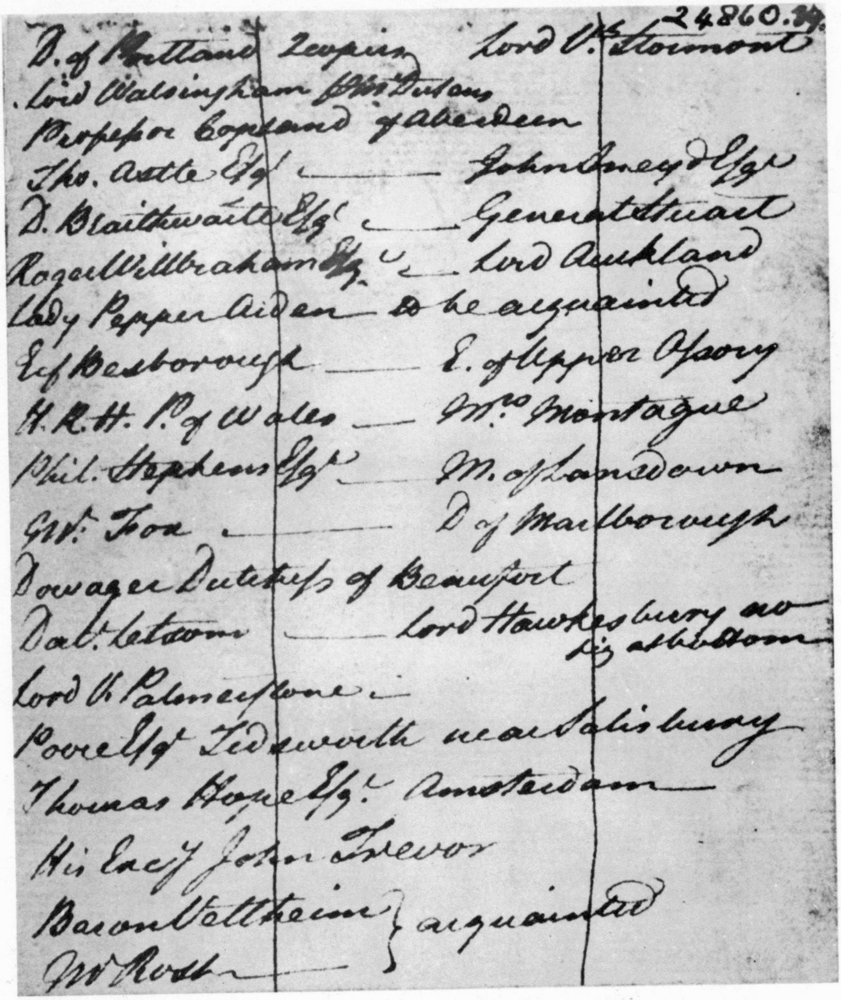

Plate XXIII

The subscribers to the first edition of Wedgwood's Portland Vase were listed by Thomas Byerley in his notebook. Though not all of them received copies, the list indicates the level of interest taken in Wedgwood's project.

Executed under the direction of J.Bell Book-seller to His Royal Highness the Prince of Wales, London April 8th. 1786.

Plate XXIV

Frontispiece to the 1786 Catalogue. Note the highly imaginative version
of the Barberini and the confusion of remarkable objects for which the
Duchess of Portland's collection was famous.

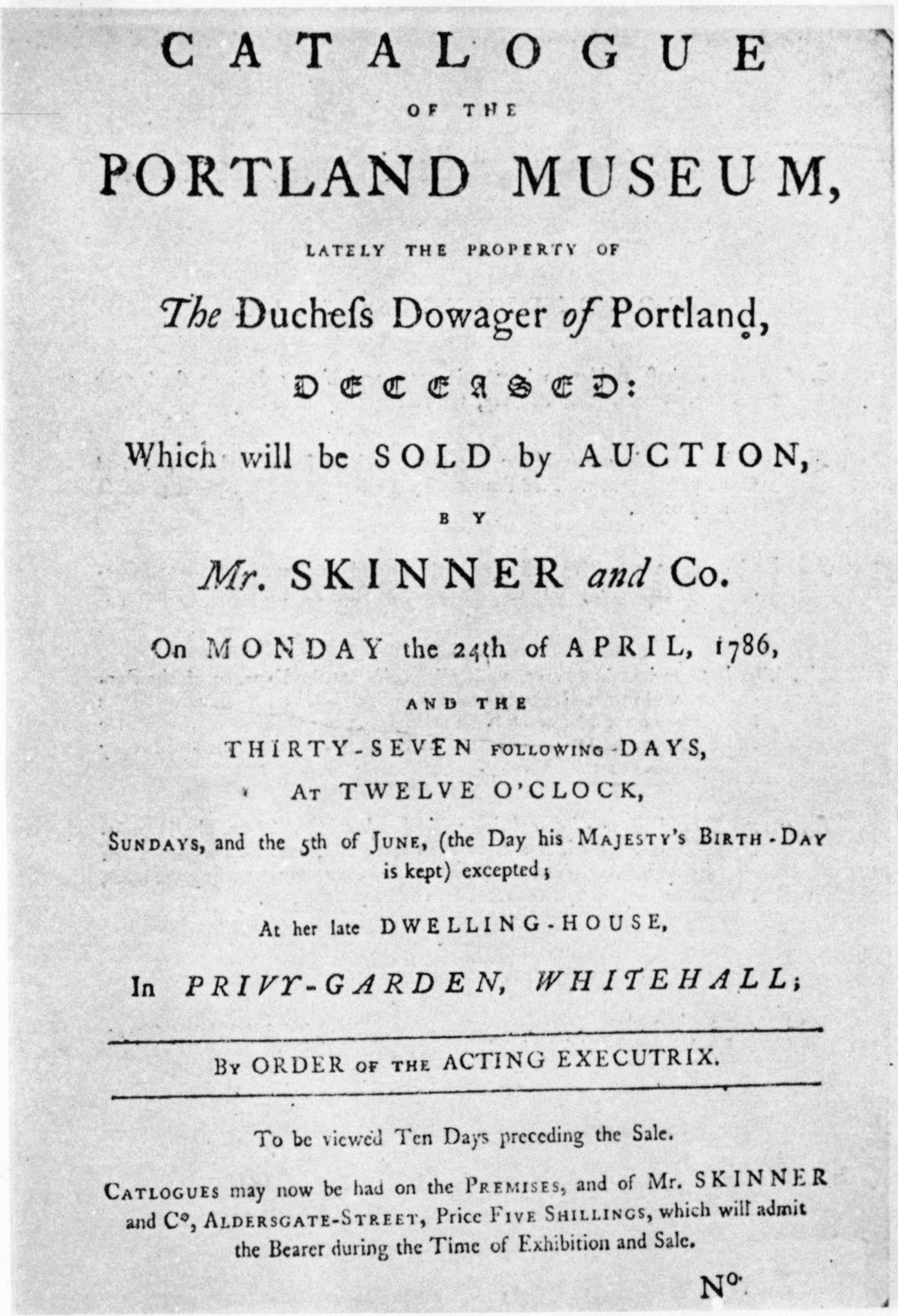

CATALOGUE

OF THE

PORTLAND MUSEUM,

LATELY THE PROPERTY OF

The Ducheſs Dowager *of* Portland,

𝔇𝔢𝔠𝔢𝔞𝔰𝔢𝔡:

Which will be SOLD by AUCTION,

B Y

Mr. SKINNER *and* Co.

On MONDAY the 24th of APRIL, 1786,

AND THE

THIRTY-SEVEN FOLLOWING DAYS,

AT TWELVE O'CLOCK,

SUNDAYS, and the 5th of JUNE, (the Day his MAJESTY'S BIRTH-DAY
is kept) excepted;

At her late DWELLING-HOUSE,

In *PRIVY-GARDEN, WHITEHALL;*

BY ORDER OF THE ACTING EXECUTRIX.

To be viewed Ten Days preceding the Sale.

CATLOGUES may now be had on the PREMISES, and of Mr. SKINNER
and Cº, ALDERSGATE-STREET, Price FIVE SHILLINGS, which will admit
the Bearer during the Time of Exhibition and Sale.

Nº.

Plate XXV

Title page of the Catalogue of the Whitehall Gardens auction, at which
the Barberini was bought by the Duke of Portland.